People, Fish and Whales

People, Fish and Whales

Dr. Murray A. Newman CM OBC
with Dr. John Nightingale

Harbour Publishing

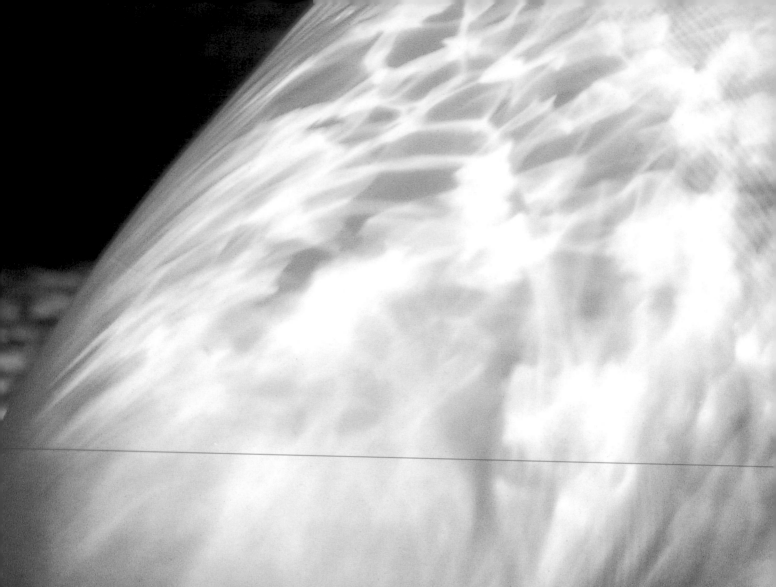

Page 1:
Busy sea otters are among
the most entertaining of the
Aquarium's exhibits. *Al Harvey*

Pages 2-3:
Curious beluga whales seem
especially interested in young
visitors. *Margaret Butschler*

These pages:
Belugas are gentle and curious
giants of the Arctic.
Noel Hendrickson

Pages 6-7:
Spectacular Pacific Canada
Pavilion displays marine life
common to the Strait of Georgia.
Hans Sipma

Pages 8-9:
Tag, the Aquarium's 787-kg
Steller sea lion, is a great
ambassador for his threatened
wild counterparts.
Noel Hendrickson

CONTENTS

INTRODUCTION
The Little Aquarium that Could

Many first-time visitors to Vancouver are surprised—and delighted—to find that it possesses one civic institution that is unquestionably among the very best in the world: its aquarium.

The Vancouver Aquarium covers an area of 0.85 hectares, making it the largest aquarium in Canada. But its physical footprint is not its most impressive statistic. There are more than 70,000 animals at the Aquarium, with about 300 separate species of fish, 230 of invertebrates, 66 of reptile and amphibian, and several bird and mammal species. This huge living community is housed in habitats and pools that hold a total of 9.5 million litres of water. By comparison, the New York Aquarium houses 350 species in 7.2 million litres of water and the London Aquarium has 350 species in 2 million litres of water.

Among the Vancouver Aquarium's special features are the BC Wild Coast display, a 4-million-litre exhibit offering close viewing of dolphins, seals, sea lions, sea otters and other typical sea life from the Pacific Northwest in a realistic outdoor setting; the Arctic Canada Gallery, featuring a 2-million-litre pool that is home to a colony of beluga whales; the Pacific Canada Pavilion, a spectacular 260,000-litre exhibit profiling the marine life of the Strait of Georgia; and the Tropic Zone, a simulated tropical rainforest featuring caimans, marmosets, sloths, birds, fish and tropical vegetation in a controlled atmosphere complete with multimedia effects. The Aquarium has 300 full-time employees and more than 800 active volunteers, including 150 youth. Almost a million visitors pass through its door each year. But the statistics tell only part of the story. In addition to its on-site displays, the Vancouver Aquarium is a hive of sophisticated programs that play active roles in education, scientific research, conservation and wild animal rescue.

Awestruck visitors on their first visit to the Vancouver Aquarium invariably ask, "How did Vancouver come to possess one of the world's great aquariums?" The answer to this question is contained in the pages that follow, and it is one of the most delightful stories in the annals of aquarium history.

Part of the answer is that the Vancouver Aquarium is located on the shore of one of the world's great inland seas, one teeming with diverse and impressive marine life. But that is only one factor. Many of the things that make the Vancouver Aquarium outstanding—its fabulous tropical and arctic exhibits, and its world-class educational programs, for instance—owe nothing to the productive marine environment of the region. The thing that most impressed me about the Vancouver Aquarium when I arrived to take

Yavari is the smallest of the Aquarium's five two-toed sloths.
Noel Hendrickson

The air-breathing giant arapaima in the Amazon Gallery boasts a hulking weight of 200 kg.
Noel Hendrickson

over as president in 1993 was—the people. I had worked in many aquariums, and many of them depended on support groups of varying sizes, but nothing prepared me for the enormous, active and dedicated legion of staff, directors, sponsors and volunteers that comprise the Vancouver Aquarium community. From its start as a non-profit society in 1950 under the leadership of the indefatigable Carl Lietze, through its building years under the leadership of a succession of visionary chairpersons aided and abetted by some of British Columbia's pre-eminent scholars and philanthropists, it has been the story of a remarkable group of people united in a vision of excellence. Not the least of those remarkable people who converged to perform this miracle on the shore of Burrard Inlet was the Aquarium's founding curator and inspired leader for its first thirty-seven years, my predecessor, Dr. Murray Newman. I can think of no more appropriate person to author this narrative of the Aquarium's first fifty years.

Dr. John Nightingale, President, Vancouver Aquarium

Above:
The Aquarium is a world-renowned centre for killer whale research, though it no longer keeps any.
John Ford

Seals are virtuoso swimmers.
Jeff Vinnick

Opposite:
Pacific white-sided dolphins are the most athletic performers in the Aquarium.
Hans Sipma

1
People

Sad-faced rockfish
make it easy to see
why people say the
aquarium's fish have
personalities.
Hans Sipma

LOOKING BACK AT THE WAY THE VANCOUVER AQUARIUM STARTED, you would never have believed one day it would be considered one of the top five aquariums in the world. I wouldn't have at first, and I was its curator. In fact, if anyone had cared to make a case that the project was doomed, I would have been Exhibit A. I had no experience. I was still a student at the University of British Columbia. My principal qualification for the new job was having briefly acted as curator of the university's fish museum. I am not sure the board members who hired me fully understood that in a fish museum, all the fish are dead. Perhaps my most important qualification was that I was willing to take the job for the paltry $400 a month they were willing to offer.

Unlike many great aquariums that were started with generous bequests or well-funded government programs, the Vancouver Aquarium was started on a shoestring by a group of enthusiastic amateurs. The ringleader was a Dutch immigrant named Carl Lietze who had been inspired by European aquariums

In the early days of the Vancouver Aquarium, the curator had to do everything. Here Murray Newman (r) fishes for new specimens using a set line with helper Dr. Jim Quayle.
Jack Long

as a boy and kept tropical fish in his basement. He and a group of fellow fish fanciers decided the time had come to build a good public aquarium in Vancouver and incorporated the Vancouver Public Aquarium Association on March 22, 1951. They consulted some experts and determined the kind of facility they envisioned could be built for $300,000. (Quite a bargain considering the Aquarium's latest improvement, the Discovery Education Centre, has a budget of $22 million.) Lietze, as president of the new society, went around to all the appropriate authorities beating his drum and received lots of lip service but no money. The Parks Board, the University of BC, the Department of Fisheries, the provincial Fish and Game Department and the community in general were eager to contribute, but in kind, not in cash.

Lack of funds threatened to kill the project before it got started. But Lietze, a successful insurance executive, was both a clever strategist and stubborn as a mule. He named the Honourable Clarence Wallace, lieutenant-governor of BC; Norman A.M. MacKenzie, president of the University of British Columbia; and H.R. MacMillan, chairman of the timber giant MacMillan Bloedel Ltd., as patrons of the association and used their good offices to get introductions to top politicians. Lietze got an audience with Vancouver mayor Fred Hume and challenged him to match any funds the aquarium group was able to get out of the provincial government. The mayor wasn't risking much by agreeing to do this because the premier of the day, W.A.C. Bennett, was notoriously tight-fisted when it came to any projects not intended to move traffic or hold back rivers. But one of the premier's favourite subjects was the degree to which the province was short-changed by the federal government. Lietze played on this and got the premier to agree that if the hated feds did the unthinkable and came across with $100,000 for an aquarium, the province would match them. No doubt Bennett felt safe, because the federal government's record for supporting cultural projects in BC was even worse than his own. But he reckoned without considering Jimmy Sinclair. The Hon. James Sinclair was the federal Member of Parliament for West Vancouver and a Liberal Party heavyweight in BC. Sinclair liked fish. In fact he was Minister of Fisheries. Lietze told him his story.

The original Aquarium building in Stanley Park was completed in 1956 at a cost of $300,000.
Dr. Bill Hoar

"So the premier promised to give you the money if I gave it to you?"

"Yep," replied Lietze.

"You got it," said Sinclair.

(It was the beginning of a beautiful friendship between Sinclair, his family and the Vancouver Aquarium. He later joined our board, his daughter Betsy served as a guide, and his son-in-law Pierre Elliott Trudeau, the prime minister of Canada, opened our new whale pool in 1971.)

After much debate over aesthetics, traffic, water quality and city park policy, the decision was made to build a single-storey aquarium in Vancouver's famous Stanley Park next to the zoo. The site was excellent, as good quality sea water could be obtained through a pipeline running to the nearby ocean, while the proximity to the already-popular zoo would be an attendance booster. This was important, because the Aquarium would be entirely self-supporting with no operational funds coming from government. Architect Ron Nairne of the firm McCarter Nairne was engaged to design a 148-by-99-foot building. Construction commenced in the spring of 1955.

By spring of 1956, construction was nearing completion. The plan was to officially open in mid-June—but how could an aquarium open if staff had not been hired and fish had not been caught? The $300,000 from the three levels of government was entirely used up to create the building and its empty displays. For the people and fish and everything that was needed to turn the bare building into a living aquarium, the board had budgeted $30,000—which seemed small to me, but the board assumed the fish could be collected free in the wild and staff could be kept to a half-dozen, as was the case for a typical zoo fish house. I wondered about this, since it seemed to me we were planning something more elaborate than a zoo fish house, but I would never have dared question the board. They were all successful men and I knew nothing about management. At board meetings I felt like a student in a classroom.

Carl Lietze (r), founding president of the Aquarium Association, appealed to Fisheries Minister James Sinclair (l) for start-up funding.
Vancouver Sun c.1956

Secretly though, I was worried. I had been on the payroll since January 1 of that year, but the board of governors did not want to hire anyone else until the last moment since it had nothing to pay them with. Even if we had staff, we did not yet have any collecting equipment, boats, trucks or facilities for them to work with. There were no labels for the specimens and the concrete tanks still needed to be washed down with vinegar so they would not poison the fish.

There was much spirited talk of fundraising to raise the hypothetical $30,000, but I couldn't see much action, other than Carl Lietze accosting every warm body he could corner to forcibly extract a $2 membership. Finally Ernie Brown, a board member who was manager of the big Hudson's Bay department store in downtown Vancouver, came forward with a plan to put on a fundraising display inside his store. We would move in portable tanks, use ice to keep the water cool; fish would be caught and transferred by provincial and federal fisheries people; UBC students would help. There was a great flurry of activity with people and trucks moving back and forth, ice spills blocking traffic, fish flip-flopping in and out of tanks, but we managed to raise $12,000. That was as close as we got to the fabled $30,000, but we stretched it far enough to cover all the furniture, equipment and start-up costs of the Aquarium. Everything else was going to have to come from gate revenues. But what if people didn't show up in the numbers required? Would we become a white elephant, as the city government feared?

I was worried.

Newman and his tiny staff had only $12,000 to furnish and stock the bare Aquarium building in 1956, but they managed.
Vancouver Aquarium Archives

The first few staff members were hired in April and May, and the federal and provincial fisheries biologists started bringing in specimens that they had netted, hooked or trawled. Staff decorated the tanks with rocks and sand; lingcod and rockfish went into the saltwater tanks; squawfish and trout into the freshwater tanks. But what about tropical tanks? Freshwater tropicals were bought at local stores, but there wasn't a saltwater tropical to be found anywhere in BC. In desperation I ordered some small clownfish and blue damselfish from a hobby store in California. They cost $300—such an exorbitant amount given our circumstances that I thought surely Lietze would seize upon it as cause to have me fired. He might have if it had been for anything but tropical fish, his favourite. Then, at the last moment, several large green sea turtles arrived from Waikiki Aquarium in Honolulu. The director there, Spencer Tinker, was aware of our seat-of-the-pants approach to stocking a major aquarium and took pity on us. The big turtles provided just the star attraction we needed for our grand opening.

I remember a last-minute panic as someone realized we were about to open our doors without an essential piece of aquarium gear nobody had thought of: a cash register. One had to be hurriedly rented downtown. Then we were ready for the big test. We had built the first true public aquarium in Canada and one of only five in North America at that time. The nearest comparable facility was the Steinhart Aquarium in San Francisco, a metropolitan area of over 1 million people. Vancouver was barely one-third that size in 1956. Was it big enough? The accountants told us we had to draw 125,000 in our first year or we'd be out of business. That meant we had to somehow pull in one person in three, a daunting thought.

Anyway, it was too late to worry about it then, and on June 15, 1956, we flung open the doors—and we were inundated. People eagerly stared into the tanks, amazed by neon tetras, angelfish and piranhas. They were excited by the dogfish, skates and salmon and awed by the big green sea turtles. Attendance the first weekend was 10,000. We got our 125,000 in the first month. I had to hire five new cashiers, drawing howls of protest from the frugal Lietze. By the year's end, a total of 340,870 people had passed through our turnstiles. We not only covered our operating costs, we were able to fund minor improvements. As the official city population at that time was 344,833, it was a remarkable feat. We published a rather cheeky promotion stating, "If you are one of those unlucky 3,963 Vancouverites who did not get around to see the fish in 1957, perhaps you will be able to make it in 1958."

Opening day, June 15, 1956. Hon. Jimmy Sinclair (r) officially opens the door while Mayor Fred Hume, President W.A. Clemens and Murray Newman look on. *Vancouver Aquarium Archives*

The Aquarium was popular right from the beginning. By the end of the first year, 340,870 people had passed through the turnstiles. *Vancouver Aquarium Archives*

AS IT TURNED OUT, VANCOUVER AND ITS NEW AQUARIUM were a match made in heaven. The entire population got behind it and made it into one of the top attractions in the country. It had many advantages that contributed to its success including its location next to one of the richest marine habitats in the world, but its greatest resource was the people of the region, who supported it in every way possible—from the civic leaders who contributed their prestige and wealth to the volunteers who tirelessly cleaned and collected to the 15,000 households that paid their annual dues and kept the turnstiles clicking. Fifty years later, the Vancouver Aquarium is still community-owned and still operationally self-supporting. Seventy-nine percent of its revenues come from admissions, memberships and services. Some 34 million visitors have passed through its portals and its annual operating budget is over $15 million.

Much credit for this goes to blessed old Carl Lietze, the bullheaded amateur aquarist who refused to give up on his dream of really *big* tanks full of tropical fish. It was he who drove the effort to sign up a huge membership, creating a strong grassroots base that has anchored the organization over the years. It was he who first allied the Aquarium with many of the region's outstanding civic leaders, commercial, political and intellectual, who have continued to give it crucial support and guidance over the years. And it was he who decided the Aquarium should hold itself up by its own bootstraps financially. This

Below:
Graphic displays helped visitors to the Aquarium understand its strange and intriguing collection of creatures. *Dominion Photo Studio, Vancouver Public Library VPL 77578D c.1963*

Above right:
In 1967 the Aquarium was tripled in size with a new high-ceilinged entrance foyer and a new dolphin pool. *Murray Newman*

Right:
View of the open foyer on a snowy day as seen across the duck pond. *Vancouver Aquarium Archives c.1972*

created a legacy of stress for several generations of administrators, but it is also one reason the Aquarium has remained dynamic and evolving. As fellow founder Dr. Bill Hoar said at the opening of the Van Dusen Aquatic Science Centre in 1980, "The most important step taken by Carl Lietze and his group was to create an atmosphere for the evolution of the aquarium idea in Stanley Park." Unlike better financed institutions that can rest on their laurels and let the endowment pay the rent, the Vancouver Aquarium has had to keep improving in order to keep the paying public coming back.

Board president Ralph Shaw, who oversaw rapid growth from 1967–71, goes head-to-head with Mister E., the world-famous mystery fish (actually a skilfish). *Gordon Sedawie / The Province*

An unexpected result of this was that even before the Vancouver Aquarium opened, I found myself thrust into the role of chief drum-beater. The various papers and radio stations in the city were curious about what we were up to, and since everybody else was busy building the place, I ended up taking the media calls. It took some getting used to, being the shy, retiring creature that I am, but with practice I developed into a passable huckster. It got to whenever there was a slow news day, editors and news directors around the city would tell their reporters, "Phone Newman and see if he has a fish story." I would always try to make their calls worthwhile. One day though, I was fresh out of wonders. The only thing in the Aquarium that hadn't already been done to death was an odd little fish with black markings like a Holstein cow recently arrived from the off-shore weather ship. We didn't even know what kind of fish it was. That gave me an idea.

"We've got a mystery fish here," I ventured.

They went for it hook, line and sinker. Mr. E, as we punningly named him, played his role to the hilt. He was quite a performer and the photographer got a shot of aquarist Bill Duncan holding one end of a fish fillet in his teeth with the plucky Mystery Fish pulling determinedly on the other end. That shot went around the world. We were in no hurry to solve the mystery of Mr. E's identity, but eventually somebody looked him up in Dr. Clemens' *Fishes of the Pacific Coast of Canada* and found he was a relatively common open sea species known as a skilfish (*Erilepis zonifer*). *Vancouver Sun* columnist Jack Wasserman once declared I was "a combination of Louis Pasteur and P.T. Barnum." This subjected

Artist's drawing for 1967 expansion shows raised entrance pavilion on right and dolphin pool in foreground. *Vancouver Aquarium Archives*

Left:
The main gallery of the original building was transformed into the H.R. MacMillan Tropical Gallery in 1967. *Murray Newman*

me to some ribbing around the boardroom, but we learned the value of good publicity early in the game, a lesson the Aquarium has never forgotten.

Actually Carl Lietze was not my favourite person, nor I his. I wasn't his choice for curator. He had backed Gerry Wanstall, a wonderfully resourceful and practical man who eventually became our chief engineer and served brilliantly in that role for many years, succeeded by John Rawle. The board overruled Carl because they wanted someone with a scholarly background to assure the Aquarium was run on sound scientific principles. This was Carl's reward for having involved a number of scientists from UBC and the Ministry of Fisheries such as Dr. Bill Hoar, Dr. Ian McTaggart-Cowan, Dr. P.A. Larkin, Dr. W.A. Clemens, Dr. C.C. Lindsey, Bob McLaren and W.R. Hourston. From the beginning the scientists insisted the Aquarium not simply wow the masses by opening the wonders of the

The famous killer whale pool under construction in 1970. With a capacity of 1.6 million litres, it set new standards for killer whale habitats.
Murray Newman

undersea world to them. They insisted it must go the further step of developing this sense of wonder into understanding and caring about aquatic ecosystems, something they knew could only be achieved by placing a strong emphasis on research and education. For this, they felt the Aquarium needed someone with scientific credentials at its head, like most of the great aquariums had.

It didn't start Carl and I off on the best footing. He was always very formal and serious with me. He always wanted more— more information, more explanation, more results. He was bossy. At one memorable meeting after I had been caught musing to a reporter about needing to enlarge the premises, he accused me of "getting too big for my britches." And I hadn't even got started then!

What probably saved my job was that just before the Aquarium opened, Lietze was replaced as president by Dr. Wilbert A. Clemens. Small and quiet as Lietze was tall and domineering, Clemens was both a distinguished ichthyologist and superb administrator. Lietze was just the kind of human bulldozer that was needed to break ground for the project, but the organizational genius of Clemens

An artist's rendering showing the growth of the Aquarium complex as of 1973. The new Finning Sea Otter Pool is in the foreground with the Killer Whale Pool, built to display Skana and Hyak in 1971, in the middle right.
Vancouver Aquarium Archives

proved the ideal follow-up to establish a smoothly running institution. I found life easier after Dr. Clemens took the chair, although Lietze continued to keep his eagle eye trained on me from his position on the board. As we grew, even he had to accept the fact we needed more staff and I was able to bring in some senior assistants who made my workload more bearable. Dmitry Stone was the first assistant curator, followed by Vince Penfold, who became curator when I was reclassified as "Director." In 1964 Gilbey Hewlett, a young UBC graduate in zoology, was hired as a biologist. Gil ultimately became curator and was for many years my right-hand man. He was with the Aquarium until finally retiring in 2006.

Six young women were hired in 1967 as uniformed guides to answer questions, deliver talks and deal with the public. This was very popular, but we couldn't afford to hire all the help we needed. This was when we came up with the idea of using docents, or trained volunteers. Art galleries used docents but the idea was new to aquariums. Joyce MacCrostie (Shives) and a group of volunteers started helping with the production of a newsletter. The Junior League became involved and provided smart, competent reinforcements to the team. We took on young men as "floor boys" to keep the floors clean and empty trash, etc., while young women worked in various areas including the Clamshell Gift Shop (where they were designated "Clamshell cuties" by the floor boys).

We soon had so many volunteers we had to get more volunteers to organize and train them. It evolved into an efficient, unpaid labour corps that contributed greatly to the Aquarium's success—and also contributed key personnel. Several floor boys went on to distinguished careers, among them our long-time assistant aquarist and author Andy Lamb and our curator of marine mammals, John Ford. One of the guides, Stefani Hewlett, became the voice of the Aquarium on CBC Radio and was elected president of the Canadian Association of Zoological Parks and Aquariums in 1985. Several of our board presidents, Jane Lawson (van Roggen), Joyce MacCrostie (Shives), Mye Wright and Lucile MacKay, rose out of the volunteer ranks. The volunteer system remains one of the outstanding features of the Vancouver Aquarium, contributing over 50,000 hours of crucial assistance each year.

I forget when it was that we stopped worrying about just surviving and started thinking about excelling. The germ had been there from the start. Lietze and his hobbyist friends had the idea of creating a proper public aquarium, not just a little fish house, though it is not clear what their vision of a proper aquarium was. The UBC contingent had, in the words of Dr. Hoar, "talked about the three essential components of a great aquarium: display, education and research." By some time in the early sixties we

Above:
Head mammal trainer Klaus Michaelis introduces killer whales Hyak and Skana to the Aquarium's new staff of whale show guide/narrators.
Ralph Bower / Vancouver Sun c. 1972

Left:
Joyce MacCrostie (Shives) helped organize the army of volunteers that made the Aquarium tick—and still does. She later became president of the Aquarium board.
Murray Newman

began to sense we had the opportunity to fulfill these aims and create something very special. I had begun travelling to curatorial symposiums around the world and had gathered a lot of exciting new ideas.

The cutting-edge museums were moving away from the traditional glass case displays to walk-through environments and other interpretive innovations that engaged all the senses. Oceanariums like Marineland of the Pacific in California had greatly expanded the traditional aquarium audience by featuring large animals such as whales, dolphins and sharks. Other biosphere-style facilities were breaking down the barriers between land, sea and air by installing ecosystem-based displays combining fish, reptiles, plants and birds, while others pursued new advances in research and education. I wanted to create a facility in Vancouver that brought all of these advances together in one place. Our dream was to build the greatest aquarium in the world.

From there, over the years, the Vancouver Aquarium grew piece by piece, gallery by gallery, until it became a major biological institution, internationally recognized for its exhibits and its programs in education, conservation and research.

By 1986 Vancouver's one-time "fish house" had evolved from its shoestring beginnings to become one of the world's great aquariums. When Dr. Murray Newman retired as Director in 1993, US aquariologist Leighton Taylor wrote, "The Vancouver Aquarium has quietly, effectively and consistently improved and influenced the aquarium profession over the past three decades. In large part such contributions are due to the consistency and commitment of a visionary yet practical executive director, who has led the institution since 1956."
Finn Larsen

AT THE END OF MARCH 1993, I RETIRED and was succeeded by Dr. John Nightingale, a dynamic and visionary aquarium veteran who had been general curator of the Seattle Aquarium and a partner in an aquarium design firm, among other things. My old Director title was dropped and Dr. Nightingale became President, while the head of the board of governors became the Chair and senior managers became Vice Presidents.

Dr. Nightingale energetically began changing the face and focus of the Aquarium. First was the renovation of the original BC Tel Pool that was located just outside the glass-walled entry hall to the Aquarium. Noted Vancouver architect Bing Thom redesigned the exhibit, bringing the pool indoors and adapting it to create the Strait of Georgia display. This new Pacific Canada Pavilion, a gift to the community from Weyerhaeuser and the Youngs, provided the Aquarium with a new "living room," as Thom called it.

In 1996 the idea of developing a salmon stream in Stanley Park was raised. The hope was to develop a stream from the Aquarium down to Coal Harbour that would support a sustainable salmon run

In 1993 Dr. John Nightingale took over the Vancouver Aquarium's reins from the retiring Dr. Murray Newman. In its first fifty years, the Aquarium only had two chief executives.
Jan Halverson

The Aquarium's signature entrance monument to killer whales, *The Chief of the Undersea World*, is a masterpiece in bronze sculpted by famed Haida artist Bill Reid. Sponsored by long-time Aquarium supporters Isabelle and Jim Graham, it was unveiled on June 2, 1984.
John Seale

so park visitors could walk along it and learn the amazing story of Pacific salmon with the help of interpretive displays. There was no natural water source available so fresh water that passes through the fresh water displays at the Aquarium was put to use. Because salmon that return to spawn home in on the scent of their native stream, a perfume-like chemical called morpholine was dripped into the water in minute amounts when the fish were young and then into the stream each fall so that they would be able to follow it back. The BC Hydro Salmon Stream opened in 2000.

The fish return to the Alcan Salmon Spawning Pool each fall where they are held until their eggs are ripe and ready for spawning. Aquarium biologists then spawn the fish and the eggs are reared in a small hatchery. An annual "Goodbye Salmon Fry" celebration is held in the spring when hundreds of children help release the young fry beginning an ocean journey that will see them returning three years later to complete the cycle.

In 2000, the Aquarium celebrated the arrival of the new millennium by redeveloping the old Sandwell Gallery as a new exhibit area called Treasures of the BC Coast. Large, lighted photographs illustrating above-water views of BC match compelling displays of BC's key underwater habitat types. The new gallery's exhibits employed a more accessible form of interpretation based on storytelling rather than the more formal scientific approach previously used. This new approach was shaped by the Aquarium's involvement in The Oceans Project (TOP), a worldwide network of over 600 aquariums, universities and agencies dedicated to raising public awareness of the aquatic environment using effective communications techniques.

In 2003, the oldest part of the Aquarium—the MacMillan Tropical Gallery—was redeveloped. Again drawing on TOP principles, the light was reduced and new interpretive displays based on the beauty and art found in tropical environments were installed. The effect was to increase emotional impact and elevate receptiveness among visitors. The renovated Tropic Zone also marked the first widespread use of computer and video technology in the Aquarium, giving visitors the opportunity to exercise their curiosity. The knowledge gathered from visitor responses to these experiments led to expanded use of new technology throughout the Aquarium.

In 2005 two donors, Vancouver businessman Rudy North and Hong Kong-based businessman David Levy, provided most of the capital ($1 million each) to revitalize and expand the research wing of the

Redtail catfish grow to an enormous size.
Margaret Butschler

Aquarium. The existing floor was rebuilt, and a second floor of labs and offices was added, while the large outdoor holding area for marine mammal research was also rebuilt. The new facility included expanded laboratories for research on local species as well as offices and labs for the marine mammal field research program and the North Pacific Marine Mammal Species at Risk Centre, which operates in partnership with the University of BC and others.

In 2005 work started on the new $22 million Education Centre, funded in part by a record private donation of $5 million from Marilyn and Stewart Blusson, a major $8.2 million grant from the Province of BC Education Centre and $3 million from Western Diversification and other federal and provincial programs. Construction was carried out under principles established by Leadership in Energy and Environmental Design (LEED), which audits everything from design to building materials to handling of demolition debris to assure a project is as green as it can be.

The new Centre includes three modern classrooms, a 145-seat theatre, conference rooms, and the Canaccord Exploration Gallery, a new public gallery with an interpretive focus that fosters exploration in Aquarium visitors. The new space allows Clownfish Cove, the pilot exhibit for very young children that has proved to be such a hit since it was opened in 2002, to be expanded and enhanced. A new feature, the Environmental Newsroom, displays environmental issues and activities from around the world on large video screens. The rest of the four floors is dedicated to offices and workspace for some of the nearly 300 full-time staff, who had been subject to increasing congestion due to 300 percent growth since 1993. The basement will contain a floor full of energy-saving equipment. Once long-term revitalization is complete, heating and cooling will be balanced across the Aquarium, drawing heat out of the beluga habitat (making it cold) and supplying it to the Tropic Zone and Amazon Gallery (warming them). This will dramatically reduce the Aquarium's energy demand for heating. LEED certification added 7 percent to the project cost, but it was agreed that to be consistent with its advocacy of marine conservation, the Aquarium should follow environmentally sound practices at all levels.

Huge two-storey Plexiglas window for the Strait of Georgia exhibition is lowered into place during building of the Pacific Canada Pavilion in 1999.
Danny Kent

The Pacific Canada Pavilion features an arresting 260,000-litre exhibit that showcases marine life of the Strait of Georgia.
Ron Sangha

A great moment: in November 2002, aquarists Mackenzie Gier and Danny Kent collect first salmon that returned to spawn in the BC Hydro Salmon Stream.
Margaret Butschler

BC Hydro Salmon Stream Project in Stanley Park

The BC Hydro Salmon Stream Project in Stanley Park is a demonstration stream running from the Aquarium to the Seawall at Coal Harbour. This is not a restoration of an existing stream but rather the creation of a stream that highlights restoration projects in the province through interactive education programs. Physically, the stream is made up of two sections. One is a recirculated freshwater portion that runs from the Children's Zoo to a log-jam just above the Alcan Salmon Pool and the other is a saltwater portion that consists of the Alcan Salmon Pool and a series of stream pools that run to Coal Harbour. A beach pump is used to pump saltwater from the ocean to create the flow of the lower stream. Each year since 1998, we have released pink, coho and chum smolts at the mouth of the stream. Since November 2001, coho have been returning successfully.

The BC Hydro Salmon Stream Project in Stanley Park was created by the Aquarium to demonstrate the life cycle of the Pacific salmon, one of nature's great wonders.
Margaret Butschler

The Wild Coast
exhibit (far right)
lets visitors get close
to coastal wildlife
in natural settings.
Left, trainer Troy
Neale and Tanya
Brown introduce
some young visitors
to the seals.
Photos Ron Sangha

Below:
In the wild, Pacific white-sided dolphins are
very social and can travel in groups of 100
or more.
Margaret Butschler

Growth of the Vancouver Aquarium

1. 1956: Vancouver Aquarium opens with 30m X 44m (1,333 sq m) building costing $300,000.

2. 1967: First major expansion, tripling Aquarium size to 4,645 sq m including BC Hall of Fishes, 568,262-litre BC Tel Pool for dolphins, Rufe Gibbs Hall of Sport Fishes and high-ceilinged entrance hall. Opened by Lt.-Gov. George Pearkes.

3. 1971: 2-million-litre Killer Whale Pool. Opened by Prime Minister Pierre Elliott Trudeau.

4. 1973: Finning Sea Otter Pool. Opened by Maury Young of Finning and Art Phillips, mayor of Vancouver.

5. 1977: 160,000-litre Gordon and Mary Russell Seal Pool. Opened by the Hon. Dr. Patrick McGeer.

6. 1980: Van Dusen Aquatic Science Centre. New labs located across rear of main building. Opened by Phae (Van Dusen) Collins.

The red Irish lord is one of the northwest's most colourful denizens.
Noel Hendrickson

7. 1983: Graham Amazon Gallery. Opened by Queen Elizabeth II and the Hon. Ron Basford.

8. 1984: Bill Reid sculpture, *The Chief of the Undersea World*. Unveiled by Lt.-Gov. Robert Rogers, Bill Reid, Guujaaw of the Council of Haida Nations, Jim and Isabelle Graham.

9. 1986: Max Bell Marine Mammal Centre opened by Carole Taylor, Jane Van Roggen and the Hon. James Richardson.

10. 1990: BC Sugar Seal Pool opened by CEO Peter Cherniavsky.

11. 1990: Arctic Canada Exhibit, 4-million-litre beluga pool with underwater viewing windows. Opened by Dr. John Webster, Hon. Titus Allooloo of the Northwest Territories, Dave Worthy MP, and Angus Ree MLA.

12. 1999: Pacific Canada Pavilion. New central exhibit featuring 2-storey Strait of Georgia tank.

13. 2000: BC Hydro Salmon Stream Project and BC Forest Headwaters Project.

14. 2001: Wild Coast Exhibit, old killer whale pool renovated to offer close observation of sea lions, dolphins, seals, otters, etc., of outer BC coast.

15. 2004 and 2006: Doubling of research wing and outdoor off-exhibit research facilities.

16. 2006: Discovery Education Centre.

2
Fish

Sockeye salmon turn
flaming red when
they return to their
home waters to
spawn.
Danny Kent

AN AQUARIUM IS SOMETHING LIKE AN ICEBERG; most of it is hidden from view. An old hand like me can walk around the Vancouver Aquarium and "read" it not only in terms of what is going on behind the scenes today, but in terms of what went before, as we grew organically, shaped by the knowledge and necessities of the moment, just as a coral reef is shaped by the currents of the constantly changing ocean.

Possibly the biggest difference in the way the Aquarium appears to an occasional visitor and those of us who live with it is in the way we are aware of its constant ebb and flow. Those who have only a momentary glance of the animals in their tanks get a rather static picture, but anyone there on a daily basis knows it as a dynamic place rippling with its own unending cycles.

As we wrote in the old *Vancouver Public Aquarium Guide*:

> People say our fish have personalities. They eat and breathe, play and fight and fall in love. Some of them carry out the wondrous cycle of birth and death.

> They do these things just as they do in their natural waters, but here you can watch them. As you do so, we hope you will share the delight we feel in their colour, beauty and activity.

> Some of you think of fish in terms of tin cans and frying pans, and for that reason the common varieties are given equal prominence with the more exotic fishes.

> Many of our visitors are neither beginners nor experts. They are simply people who like fish. Some of them come again and again, and they tell us that the silent creatures of the sea teach them of beauty and tranquility not often found in this hurried life.

Above: Indo-pacific tropical fishes, such as this giant humpbacked wrasse and this orange-striped triggerfish are uniquely shaped and marked. *Photos Margaret Butschler*

Left: Some piranhas relatives eat only fruit and nuts, but the red-bellied piranha in the Amazon Gallery are flesh eaters. Carnivorous piranhas can devour large prey such as cows and humans by tearing them to bits with their triangular blade-like teeth. *Paddy Ryan / Ryan Photographic*

Opposite: Adult male wolf eels are fierce with each other but are readily tamed to accept handouts by divers. *Phil Edgell*

Top (left to right):
The giant sunflower
star is a voracious
and swift predator. It
is the largest sea star
on the planet.
Bernie Hanby

The black-eyed
hermit crab has
large, black, almond-
shaped eyes that are
hard to miss.
Phil Edgell

The basket star
has five cleverly
camouflaged arms,
which it extends
to form a deadly
basket-like cage.
Doug Pemberton

There was a very large psychiatric hospital called Essondale in the Vancouver area in the 1950s and 60s and the Aquarium became one of its favourite diversions. Sometimes the galleries would be totally filled with patients, moving silently and slowly along in front of the tanks. The "silent creatures of the sea" had a powerful effect on them. Nurses told us when patients returned to the hospital they would talk about the creatures and write about them—even draw pictures of them. There's no doubt they got a lot more out of their visits than many of our patrons, who seem to have trouble slowing down to the fishes' pace.

Watching the animals in the Aquarium can be fascinating if you take the time to study them. The marine invertebrates are so strange and ancient and beautiful, particularly those of the coast of British Columbia, where they are so numerous and diverse. The giant multi-armed sunflower star, with its puffy orange flesh and wiggling tube feet, has over its surface tiny pincers that ward off larval organisms that might settle there. This sunflower is predatory and rather swift-moving. Prey animals such as scallops escape by snapping their shells and swimming away. Even some anemones are able to escape by tumbling away.

Red-gilled
nudibranch. The
word nudibranch
means "naked gills."
There are more than
200 colourful species
of nudibranchs or
sea slugs in the
Pacific Northwest.
Doug Pemberton

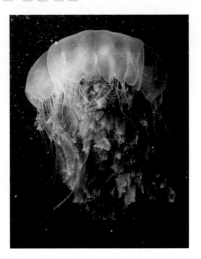

Large, delicate-looking anemones are common in BC waters. The plumose anemone can be orange or white or beige in colour. Sometimes in the Aquarium they are collapsed into a small mass on a rock, but if you give them time you will see them extend lacy plumes covered with tiny stinging cells around their mouths as they go about capturing their planktonic prey.

The fish tend to watch each other. Some are passive, some are predatory, some are potential prey, some form schools, some are solitary and some are aggressive toward each other. Some fish seek protection by swimming alongside large fish. Other fish hide in rocks or under the sand. Fingerling coho salmon and rainbow trout set up social hierarchies or "pecking orders" from very dominant individuals to very subordinate ones. It is fun to observe the fish carefully because they are so different from each other and their ways of behaving are so diverse.

Top (left to right):
When seen in the Aquarium plumose anemones are sometimes collapsed into unattractive lumps but will extend lacy plumes if given time.
Margaret Butschler

The Pacific Northwest is home to many varieties of shrimp.
Margaret Butschler

The lion's mane jellyfish has stinging tentacles that can stretch to 9 metres.
Bernie Hanby

The lingcod, one of the many fish on display in the Pacific Canada Pavilion, is a species at risk in the Strait of Georgia.
Lee Newman

Sea otters are perhaps easier to watch because they keep so busy. They are among the only tool-using animals in this part of the world. They love to float on their backs and eat sea urchins, which they place on their bellies and hammer open with a rock held in both hands. Sometimes in the Aquarium they develop the bad habit of lifting up a rock and hammering very hard against the glass, even breaking it on occasion. Though chubby-looking in their thick fur coats, their bodies are actually rather thin. Unlike seals, they have no insulating layer of blubber and depend upon their heavy fur remaining clean and dry on the inside. For this reason they must spend much of their day grooming and "blow-drying" themselves—they blow on their fur to make a warm air pocket next to their skin.

A sea otter's fur is one of nature's wonders. It has 100,000 hairs per square centimetre, which comes to almost a billion hairs per animal. It is perhaps the finest fur in the animal kingdom, and that was almost

their undoing. When the British explorer James Cook became the first European to reach BC in 1778 he was so impressed with the sea otter fur cloaks worn by First Nations people of the outer coast he bartered for some hides to trade in China. They were such a hit with the Chinese a fur trade sprung up that caused the sea otter to be hunted to extinction on the coast of BC by the mid-1800s. In an effort to revive the BC population, eighty-nine otters were transplanted from Alaska to the west coast of Vancouver Island between 1969 and 1972 and by 2003 this colony had grown to about 3,000. It is one of the few success stories where an extinct population has "come back from the dead" in BC.

Top:
Using its belly as a dinner table, the sea otter uses a rock to smash open the tasty crab or sea urchin.
Jeff Vinnick

Above:
Sea otters spend much of their lives floating on their backs.
Margaret Butschler

Right:
Sea otters spend much of their day grooming and "blow-drying" themselves—they blow on their fur to make a warm air pocket next to their skin.
Bob Herger

The sea otter has one of the finest coats in the animal kingdom, boasting almost 100,000 hairs per square centimetre.
Noel Hendrickson

Milo enjoys a tasty feast of sea urchin. The sea otter is one of the most ravenous eaters in the Aquarium, and will burn through 30 percent of its body weight in fresh seafood every day.
Margaret Butschler

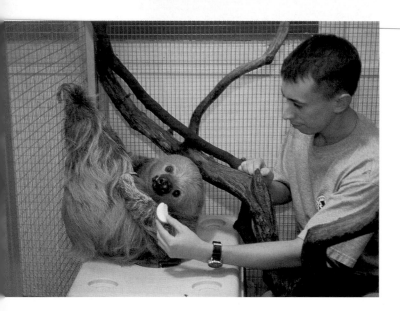

Above: Aquarist Mike Delaney offers a tasty tidbit to Orinoco the sloth.
Ron Sangha

Above right: Trainer Billy Lasby prepares a feast of herring for the Steller sea lions.
Noel Hendrickson

Right: Aquarist Sharon Jeffery prepares the daily seafood dinner for the Aquarium animals. All the seafood served at the Aquarium is fit for human consumption.
Ron Sangha

HAVING ANIMALS IN AN AQUARIUM PRESENTS AN OPPORTUNITY to witness actions impossible to see in nature. The longer you can spend observing, the more you will be rewarded with unexpected and fascinating behaviour as the creatures act out their natural cycles.

The most common cycle is the feeding cycle. An aquarium is, among other things, a huge seafood restaurant. The Marine Mammal Department has a massive seven-tonne freezer. Incredibly, seventy-five tonnes of herring pass through this freezer every year. It costs about $150,000 annually to feed the marine mammals at the Aquarium. The cost is allocated as follows: $9,500 on vitamins, $20,000 on squid, $25,000 on fish fillets, $30,000 on shellfish and $60,000 on herring. The whales' and dolphins' diets must be supplemented because some vitamins naturally degenerate in the frozen fish they are fed and must be replaced to ensure the animals' health. Sea otters refuse to eat vitamins, so they are fed a wider range of foods to ensure their health. A second freezer has a capacity of eight tonnes, and holds food for all of the animals except birds, mammals and marine mammals. In this freezer you will find krill, shrimp, smelt, herring and clams among other foods. All of the seafood used at the Aquarium is fit for human consumption.

Every creature the Aquarium takes on comes with a grocery list and a feeding schedule that becomes one more duty for the busy keepers. Some animals can go days without food while others eat non-stop. When we first started we placed the care and feeding of the tropical fish in the hands of a gentleman who was represented to me as an expert, and in a very short time he allowed much of the display to fall sick and die. To fill the position provisionally I borrowed a nineteen-year-old assistant named Billy Wong from his father's pet store—and he stayed with us thirty-five years, rising in time to the position of chief aquarist. Billy soon nursed the fish tanks back to health, being careful to avoid the error of over-feeding that besets many beginners, but in time we began to feel some of the tropicals weren't doing as well as they might be. We were feeding them only twice a week. When we hired a new assistant aquarist in 1968, Klaus Michaelis (later head mammal trainer), he came up with a new theory: maybe we should feed them more often, since in their natural habitat coral reef fish are constantly

Above:
Billy Wong came over from his father's pet shop to provide temporary help and stayed 35 years, rising to chief aquarist.
Murray Newman

Left:
Feeding the sharks is a task best approached with care—and long tongs.
Noel Hendrickson

nibbling. So we started feeding more often, but in small amounts, and the fish did better. In those days there was really nobody to ask, so we had to work these things out through trial and error. Our goal was to attain the highest possible standard of animal care and in this we were quite successful. In 1975, we became the first aquarium accredited by the American Zoo and Aquarium Association (AZA). The Aquarium is also accredited by the Canadian Association of Zoos and Aquariums (CAZA) and in 1987 was designated Canada's Pacific National Aquarium by the Canadian government.

The sea otter is one of the most ravenous eaters in the Aquarium. It relies on a high metabolic rate to maintain its body heat in the cold sea water, with the result that it burns through 30 percent of its body weight in fresh seafood every day. The octopus is another big eater. Starting from a barely visible hatchling, it can grow to a massive adult weighing fifty kilograms in the space of three years, using its powerful beak to break open crabs and other shellfish. Sloths are at the opposite extreme. Sluggish and slow to metabolize, they can take more than a week to digest a single meal.

As careful as we were to feed our charges the right things, we had to be just as watchful of their tendencies to snack on the wrong things—like each other. Certain fish tend to be very nippy, and not always the ones you'd expect. When we placed our first three lemon sharks in the newly renovated Caribbean pool in 1971, our resident school of tasty little jacks dropped from eleven to one overnight—not so surprisingly. There was also a chunky little jewfish in the tank that we were afraid might end up as an hors d'oeuvre, but she turned the tables on the sharks and began munching on their tails and fins so determinedly we had to remove her for *their* protection.

Cuddles the crocodile required surgery after swallowing 3 pounds of pennies. Vancouver Aquarium Archives

Our crocodiles gave us some headaches with their tendency for inappropriate grazing—though not on paying customers, thankfully. The largest croc, a five-foot male named Cuddles, went off his grub one time and was found to have an unidentified mass the size of a grapefruit lodged in his digestive tract. We tried purgatives without success, and finally took him to Dr. Roberta Hartman's Cove Animal Clinic for surgery. An important fact to keep in mind when operating on crocodiles is that anaesthetics don't faze them. But being cold-blooded, the cooler they get the more sluggish they become and if you keep cooling them down until they are immobile you can work on them safely. The hardest part was sawing through Cuddles' tough outer armour. Once inside, Dr. Roberta reached in and brought out a handful of . . . pennies. Then another, and another, until she had three pounds worth. Visitors had been using the alligator pool as a wishing well, and Cuddles had been discreetly stowing away the proceeds—perhaps saving for a trip to the Mexican swamps of his origin. Once buttoned up— literally, since Roberta had to use steel wire anchored to buttons to pull Cuddles' thick belly plates back together—it wasn't long before the big fellow was back in his pool ravenously attacking his portion of horse heart and trying to get at the turtles in the adjoining pen.

What does the Aquarium feed the animals, and where do they get the food?

To keep the animals healthy it is necessary to feed them a wide variety of nourishing food. Most of their food is purchased from local fishers and food suppliers. Some is even bought at regular grocery stores! Here's a few examples of what Aquarium animals eat:

- Barnacles: fish, seaweed, brine shrimp
- Octopuses: crabs, herring
- Fishes: brine shrimp, plankton, fresh lettuce, chopped smelt, cod fillets, herring
- Sharks: mackerel, smelt, herring and squid
- Beluga whales: herring, capelin, squid
- Lizards: fruit, vegetables, meal worms, crickets
- Seals: herring
- Sea otters: fish fillets, squid, crabs, clams
- Steller sea lions: herring, squid, capelin
- Sea stars: clams, herring

When beluga whales give birth, powerful contractions push the baby out tail first. Natural reproduction is the best way to maintain the aquarium collection.
Jeff Vinnick

Below:
Redfoot tortoise with offspring.
Margaret Butschler

THEN THERE ARE THE LIFE CYCLES. The specimens in the collection are continuously aging, dying and being born, all according to their own biological clocks. You might think the greatest creatures are the longest lived and vice versa, but looks can deceive. Rockfishes, which are among the smaller fishes, are among the longest lived of all the Aquarium's tenants, living more than a century. On the other hand, the giant Pacific octopus only lives three to four years. Like a salmon, it dies after reproducing. One of the Aquarium's most massive residents, thirty-six-year-old beluga Kavna, is a certified senior citizen who has the distinction of being the longest-lived beluga in a North American aquarium. Almost reaching prime at thirty-six, Gino, the double yellow head Amazon parrot in the Amazon gallery, is another one of the Aquarium's longer-lived species. These wildly differing expiry dates present curatorial staff with a special challenge. An aquarium that decides to display an octopus, for instance, can't think in terms of collecting just one; it must think it terms of establishing a continuous supply. To some degree, this is true of every specimen it exhibits.

The ideal source of new specimens is to have the old ones reproduce within the Aquarium. It was a great day when the young beluga Aurora delivered a healthy calf, Qila, in 1995, and again when she delivered her second offspring, Tuaq, in 2002. Successful births within the Aquarium walls provide continuity without the expense—and without the controversy, in the case of whales—of obtaining replacements from the wild. Natural births are welcomed by the staff because most animals don't breed if they are unhealthy or stressed, and natural birth is the best proof your charges are thriving. Mating behaviour is a sign of healthy, well-adjusted animals as well as a great attention-grabber. When Hyak and Skana, our two massive killer whales, engaged in sexual behaviour, the public was often amazed by what they saw.

Above:
Older and younger Steller sea lions sunbathe at the Aquarium.
Hans Sipma

The sea otters were among the most sexually aggressive animals on display. We soon learned that if two male sea otters were housed with a female, the males would fight. On the other hand, a group of females can co-exist with one male. When we presented our first otter, John, with two new females from Alaska named Attu and Kiska, he immediately attempted to mate with both of them. Later, he settled down to mating only (but frequently!) with Kiska. If she was on a platform, he would often try to drag her back into the water, tugging at her tail with his forepaws. Occasionally she initiated the play, either by sniffing or (less subtly) by leaping on him. There would be much splashing and rolling about in the water and it would continue for as long as twenty minutes off and on. Male otters, being larger than females, are very rough in their mating behaviour. They often bite the upper part of the female's nose during copulation, causing bleeding. Some of our staff—I won't mention which gender—reacted quite strongly to this, feeling the males were unduly brutal. However, the birth of furry little babies mollified their sensitivities. We learned a lot about breeding sea otters in those years, and had raised ten healthy offspring by the late 1980s. The Vancouver Aquarium has been a net exporter of sea otters, providing animals to aquariums as far away as Japan, where the family continues to grow.

Diver Ken O'Neil with a 30-kg octopus he caught for the Aquarium in 1960. Volunteer collectors were a great help.
Murray Newman

SOME SPECIES NATURALLY BREED PROLIFICALLY and are always in surplus, while others simply can't reproduce in captivity, and all are prone to accident and disease, just as they are in the wild, so maintaining the collection with replacements from outside sources is a key activity at any aquarium. A gratifying amount of this can be achieved by exchanges between aquariums—curators are great traders—but collecting from the wild is still the mainstay of most aquatic collections.

From the beginning it was obvious we needed our own collecting boat. The federal ministry of fisheries and provincial fish and game people had saved our bacon by pitching in to fill our tanks at first, and several commercial fishermen and divers had been a great source of help, but we couldn't impose on them indefinitely. With some expert help in 1959 we found the *Aquarius*, a double-ended thirty-foot ex-fishboat. The *Aquarius* had a live tank, which meant a previous owner had fitted her for transporting fish live to market by flooding part of the hull and letting sea water flow in and out through holes in the bottom. This should have been just the thing for our work, but there was a glitch. The live tank was sealed off from the rest of the boat by watertight bulkheads, which prevented the holes in the bottom from flooding the whole boat and making it sink. In theory. In practice, the bulkheads weren't as tight as they needed to be. We collected a lot of sea life with the *Aquarius*, but we also had to collect the boat itself fairly frequently—from the bottom of its mooring in False Creek. It was later replaced by the more buoyant twenty-eight-footer, *Nautichthys*, operated for many years by our assistant chief aquarist,

In 1986, aquarist Philip Bruecker gathered sea stars and other specimens while diving from the collecting vessel *Aquarius*.
Murray Newman

Andy Lamb, who in 1970 alone made eighteen collecting expeditions in BC waters, setting lines and diving for all manner of fish and invertebrates. In 2004 the Aquarium christened a new twenty-five-foot research and collecting boat the *Rudy N,* after long-time supporter Rudy North. A versatile, well-equipped vessel that can be trailered to far-flung parts of the coast, it keeps busy under the able direction of Curator of BC Waters Danny Kent.

This of course only addresses the problem of how to stock local fish. Since much of our collection consisted of exotic species from around the world, the question of how we were to maintain this part of the collection arose early on. Part of the answer came one fine day while the Vancouver Aquarium was still in the talking stages. I was walking past the old biological sciences building at UBC when my professor Bill Hoar stuck his head out the window.

"How would you like to go on a collecting trip to Mexico?" he said.

"When do we go?" I asked.

"Tomorrow," he said.

The timber magnate H.R. MacMillan was taking his 137-foot yacht *Marijean* to Acapulco and wanted a fish expert to go along as ship's naturalist, cruising the Pacific coast with him and his family for a month. Well, somebody had to do it, and I was able to persuade my wife Kathy of the scientific importance of my

Top:
Aquarium biologist Andy Lamb with a spiny dogfish. Andy joined the Aquarium staff in the 1960s and became a noted author and teacher.
Murray Newman

Above:
The Aquarium's old collecting truck sometimes ventured as far afield as California.
Don Wilkie

Left:
The Aquarium's first collecting boat was an ex-fishboat named the *Aquarius* that had a penchant for sinking.
Murray Newman

presence, so after some panicky rescheduling, off I went. I must have earned my keep, because I was invited back the following year and every succeeding year until the *Marijean* was sold in 1967. These expeditions became an important source of supply for the Aquarium's tropical collections, once even providing us with a twelve-foot manta ray (frozen). Not only that, H.R. MacMillan became a major sponsor of the Aquarium, as did his family, particularly his daughter Jean Southam.

Pleasant as I found the cruising and collecting, bringing live fish back from Mexico was a big headache. It seldom worked out that the ship was returning when I was, so I had to bring my samples home by plane. First I had to move them from Acapulco to Mexico City via small plane, then transship them to Vancouver via commercial airline. I remember once following the fish to Mexico City on a second plane only to learn that the boxes had been diverted to a warehouse somewhere. I rushed madly around sprawling Mexico City and finally found the boxes but the fish were getting cold, so I had to warm them up. They also needed more oxygen by that time so all the plastic bags carrying the sea water and fish had to be opened. Oxygen tanks were found, the bags were oxygenated then tied up, repacked and shipped off to Vancouver where the Aquarium team anxiously awaited. The fish survived in better condition than I did.

Mexican waters were productive, but more of our tropical fishes came from South America. The Amazon basin contains the largest range of freshwater fish in the world. At least 1,300 species have been identified, among them some of the world's most fascinating fish. Piranhas are the best known, but there are also gigantic catfish and massive air-breathing arapaimas, freshwater sharks and stingrays,

Below:
H.R. MacMillan (second from left) was the founder of Canada's largest forestry company, MacMillan Bloedel, and a generous benefactor of the Aquarium.
Murray Newman

Below right:
Some of the Aquarium's most important early collecting took place in tropical waters aboard timber magnate H.R. MacMillan's yacht *Marijean*.
Murray Newman

A diver collects specimens in the south Pacific.
Murray Newman

little hatchet fish that glide over the surface like flying fish, brilliantly coloured tetras, characins with heavy teeth for cracking nuts, and four-eyed fish called *Anableps* that see above and below the water at the same time.

It occurred to me an expedition to the Amazon region might be justified as a way to enlarge our collection, learn more about the natural history of Amazon fishes and generate publicity for the Aquarium. I presented my idea to the board, but they turned it down, saying we could buy the fish much cheaper from pet stores. I kept thinking about the Amazon, however, and events conspired to move it up on the public agenda. During the late 1970s the Amazon basin, with its great rainforest subject to ever-increasing pressure from cattle farming and industry, was placed in the spotlight by a global environmental campaign that characterized it as "the lungs of the earth." By this time Jim and Isabelle Graham, an adventurous Vancouver couple with time and money to spend on things that interested them, had become involved in Aquarium expeditions to Africa and the Arctic and offered to help fund a major exhibit on the Amazon. Isabelle had a particular interest in birds, so we decided to make it an ecological exhibit showing the interdependence of plants and animals of the water, land and air.

Accompanied by the Grahams, I finally set out for the Amazon in 1979, starting at the headwaters in the Peruvian Andes, then moving down to the Peruvian lowlands and into Brazil. Aided by Robin Best, a young Vancouver scientist working in Brazil, we cruised down the dark waters of the Rio Negro and then up the cloudy Amazon itself where we caught amazing samples of armoured catfish, silvery

The Indo-Pacific exhibit presents an amazingly complex tropical habitat.
Hans Sipma

arawanas and colourful peacock cichlids. Over the next several years there were more expeditions and much conferring with other aquariums before the Graham Amazon Gallery finally opened on March 9, 1983. By good fortune we were able to have the opening officiated by Queen Elizabeth II, which caused a great flurry and brought out 5,000 people. Isabelle, Jim and I had the honour of showing Her Majesty around the new exhibit while staff peeked out from corners like jungle animals.

I kept wanting to point things out, but a protocol person had sternly warned me not to initiate conversation, and above all, not to point. The Queen first inspected the giant arapaima rising and falling in its tank, then the caimans lounging like miniature crocodiles on our simulated riverbank. Our simulated tropical thunderstorm came on at the right moment with its impressive thunder and lightning. We passed the video display showing that the Amazon rainforest was being destroyed. Everything was going perfectly. Then I forgot myself and raising my arm to point, blurted out, "Oh look, there's the sloth!" Whatever dire consequences might have ensued from this *faux pas* were overtaken by the appearance of our two marmosets. Arguably the cutest creatures in creation, these small monkeys often hide in the foliage but ventured out to peer curiously at the Queen, as she paused to peer back at them. She stood lost in the wonder of nature for several beats before remembering herself and resuming her measured pace. It was one of those moments that stay with you down the years.

"The operation of an aquarium like this is one of the livelier arts," I was quoted as saying in a 1959 magazine article. "Try combining the essential features of a department store, school, fish hatchery with a plumber's nightmare and a wild animal circus which runs full-time." I was only at the outset of my curatorial career when I formulated that capsule description of the work, but after thirty years' further experience, I would have been hard-pressed to improve upon it. What I didn't foresee was how quickly the Vancouver Aquarium would graduate from being the new kid on the block, begging advice and assistance from experts like Spencer Tinker of the Waikiki Aquarium and Earl Herald of the Steinhart Aquarium, to the position where we ourselves became recognized as experts, and our staff was being asked to consult on newer aquariums like the Port of Nagoya Public Aquarium and the Monterey Bay Aquarium.

Left:
The sloths are very difficult to spot because they rarely move. Their tawny colour is the perfect camouflage.
Margaret Butschler

Below right:
One of the Aquarium's prized scarlet ibises.
Vici Johnstone

Above left:
Beginning in June the Aquarium releases 400 butterflies a week into the Amazon Gallery.
Margaret Butschler

Left:
The Aquarium is home to a group of crocodilians.
Margaret Butschler

3
Whales

Until the Vancouver Aquarium captured the first live killer whale in 1964, *Orcinus orca* were thought to be bloodthirsty villains of the sea, dangerous to get near even in a boat. The Aquarium proved otherwise.

Finn Larsen

Above:
In 1967 the Aquarium installed Skana, its first on-site killer whale, in the BC Tel Dolphin Pool.
Murray Newman

Right:.
A quick learner, Skana contained her dislike of skinny people and gave Prime Minister Trudeau a nice spy-hop when he opened the new Killer Whale Pool in 1971.
Pierre Dow

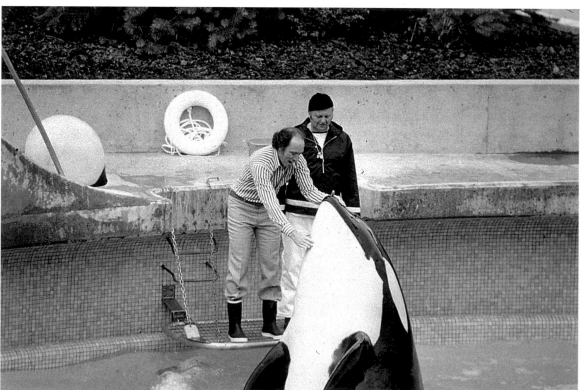

While it lasted, the killer whale display was a great success. The whale shows drew huge crowds and fuelled three decades of expansion, starting with the new $1.5 million whale pool opened by Prime Minister Trudeau in 1971. With huge Plexiglas windows for underwater viewing, this spacious 1.6-million-litre complex set new standards for cetacean displays. In 1986 we upgraded the whale pool, creating the four-million-litre Max Bell Marine Mammal Centre, which placed emphasis on the environment and biology of the orca rather than the show performance. This trail-blazing design became a model whose influence can be seen in many parts of the aquarium community.

Killer whales proved to be very interesting animals. They were endlessly good-natured, seldom showing aggressiveness toward their keepers even in times of great stress, such as when we drained the pools for medical examinations or when an underwater viewing window blew out during one of Skana's jumps, causing her to be sucked through the opening up to her blowhole and cut for 120 stitches. Our staff enjoyed diving with Skana. She clearly liked the companionship and let them hitch a free ride holding onto her dorsal fin from time to time. Her most endearing habit was "holding hands," an activity she initiated herself by squeezing the diver's hand between her flipper and her side and slowly swimming around the pool. It was delightful, but we never lost sight of what a formidable predator we were dealing with. One morning we found Splasher, our first dolphin, at the surface of the pool, dying. He sometimes angered Skana with his aggressive behaviour, and apparently she had crushed him against the side of the habitat. Skana was the unchallenged head of the pool hierarchy. If something interesting fell into the water, she would always end up with it. She insisted on having first go at everything. In the wild, females head the basic family units, or matrilines.

Skana seemed to enjoy performing before an audience more than any other whale we ever had. If the stands were crowded and people were clapping loudly, she'd jump higher than on a slow day. For most

The killer whale shows drew huge crowds and transformed the once-despised orca into a symbol of all that was good and pure in West Coast nature.
Brian Kent / Vancouver Sun

of her thirteen years in the Aquarium she seldom refused to perform as long as the routine remained exactly the same. As she grew older, she became very fixed in her ways. Once, trainer Klaus Michaelis tried to teach her to roll over and when he leaned down to give her a herring she rose up and clamped his head in her toothy jaws—gently, but firmly enough for a pointed warning. After that, trainers seldom tried to make Skana do anything new. She had other quirks. Like all killer whales, she could spit, and a killer whale pa-tooie can drench you from head to foot. The trainers felt that, perhaps because of her own matronly girth, she didn't like thin people. Our staff held its collective breath at the grand opening of the whale pool in 1971 when Prime Minister Pierre Elliott Trudeau, a famously lean specimen, decided to make a photo op of handing Skana a herring. If she had doused him, it could have been bad for our federal funding application. Instead she made a great show of rising up as if to deliver a smooch, which perhaps showed how smart she really was.

Pender Harbour fishers Sonny Reid and Bert Gooldrup provided the Aquarium with a second orca, a calf called Peanut but later known and loved by millions as Hyak.
Murray Newman

The office of the whale trainers had large acrylic windows looking into the whale pool through which they could constantly observe the whales. The whales, in turn could constantly observe the trainers. Once Jeremy Fitz-Gibbon was standing in front of a viewing window with a model of a salmon and noticed Hyak looking on with interest from the other side of the glass. He and John Ford began showing Hyak pictures from a book and when they showed pictures of killer whales, dolphins or fish, Hyak would press his eye up against the window. He would remain as long as his breath held out, about ten minutes. If they showed any other type of animal, he would drift away, but killer whale pictures brought him back. No other whale showed much interest in printed matter, but Whitewings, a Pacific white-sided dolphin, sometimes did. Once Jeremy hung up a large poster showing every species of dolphin and whale, and Whitewings ran her eye up and down the columns, carefully checking out each one.

Skana loved performing for a responsive crowd and would sometimes nip Hyak if he flubbed a routine.
Colin Savage

One quiet afternoon, long after Klaus had retired, I encountered Clint Wright, the new chief trainer, playing with Bjossa at poolside. Bjossa was staring at him like a dog waiting for his master to throw a stick. But rather than a stick, Clint would pick up a tiny pebble and toss it far out into the middle of the pool. The great whale would lunge off in pursuit and return moments later, delicately holding out this speck of stone on its lower lip. Clint was only half paying attention, obviously a little bored with the game, but I was amazed. Even after years of observing these animals, they kept astounding us.

Opinions varied among our staff members as to how intelligent killer whales are. Dr. John Ford, who spent over twenty-five years studying them for us, approaches the question cautiously. He starts by saying that while perceptive and capable of innovation, they are not intelligent in any way that resembles human intelligence. Much human intelligence is connected to vision, and though whales have about the same visual acuity as a cat, poor underwater visibility limits its use most of the time. Ford surmises they navigate as much as anything by listening to ambient beach noise, which accounts for some of the odd places they end up like Indian Arm, an offshoot of industrial, polluted Burrard Inlet. Killer whales can make an impressive range of sounds that vary from group to group so that researchers

can identify unique tribal "dialects," but that does not mean they have a language in the way humans have a language. Nor do they seem to be able to communicate about past or present events, or to process abstract ideas as humans do. But they are intelligent in their own very distinct way, and we were aware they needed environmental enrichment to keep from getting bored, so we interacted with them frequently and kept them active. The staff entertained the whales by throwing large orange floats into the pool while the whales entertained the public by jumping and splashing.

In 1972 Susan Hoffer, a young biologist studying the behaviour of the killer whales, observed that when an object such as a feather or piece of paper fell into the pool it was often taken up by either Hyak or by Diana, a female dolphin. Both would spend time vying for it until they lost interest. Diana would often even attempt to remove the object from Hyak's mouth. The relationship between the Aquarium's killer whales and the dolphins sometimes reminded you of people with their dogs. But, then, in terms of whales and dolphins, which is the person and which is the dog? Hyak and Diana were good friends. They often swam together and played with each other. After eating and participating in a whale show, the whales and dolphins would usually swim in a tight group moving slowly along together in a relaxed way around the pool as they digested their food.

Although some killer whales prey upon Pacific white-sided dolphins in the wild, they lived happily together at the Vancouver Aquarium.
Murray Newman

Behaviour between different species is always interesting to watch. Killer whales are predatory of course but they do not eat just any kind of animal. As staff scientist John Ford has shown, some of them eat fish and some eat mammals but fish-eaters do not eat mammals. In the Aquarium killer whales did not attack and eat seals or dolphins, but it was said that sometimes they would swallow a duck or seagull that landed on the surface of the pool.

In 1985 Bjossa seemed to have a relationship with a grey, juvenile glaucous-winged gull. The bird would assume the typical begging posture and call of a youngster soliciting food from an adult and wait while Bjossa approached the pool edge with a herring in her mouth. The bird would peck at the herring while the whale would hold it gingerly in her front teeth. This unusual exchange would take place every day with the whale quite deliberately offering food, and offering it only to the one bird. Bjossa feeding the gulls became a fascinating performance enjoyed by many Aquarium visitors.

Bjossa was flown in from Iceland to replace Skana and carried on her predecessor's tradition as boss lady of the whale pool (orcas are matrilineal).
David Fleetham

About a year before, Bjossa began to occasionally bite the heads off her food fish before eating the bodies. Seagulls, ever the bold scavengers, were quick to pick up the cast-off heads. As they did this, the whale would lie very still near the fish head, not disturbing the water, so that the fish head floated as long as possible before sinking out of reach of the gulls. It appears as if the gulls began to associate fish tidbits with the whale's mouth and gradually approached closer and closer until one or more were pecking at fish right in the whale's mouth. It was almost as if Bjossa was taking a page from our trainers' book, and methodically training the birds. Interestingly, casual as the seagulls became about approaching Bjossa's toothy maw, they seemed to know better than to try it with either of the male whales, who might give in to the temptation to swallow them.

In the Aquarium the whales and dolphins frequently played with their food fish, often balancing a fish on the leading edge of a flipper and letting the pressure of the flowing water hold it there. In addition, the young killer whales were seen cooperating as one took bites of fish held in the other animal's mouth. We speculated that this may be a kind of feeding behaviour that more typically would take place between mothers and calves, in the same way that the mother sea otters begin offering solid food to their pups as early as three weeks of age.

Trainer Jeremy Fitz-Gibbon believed Hyak liked to browse books through the underwater viewing window—as long as there were pictures of tasty salmon or other killer whales.
Finn Larsen

Why did the Aquarium choose to end its killer whale program? There were a number of reasons. In most ways orcas adapted well to life in captivity. In the early years, they didn't live as long as in the wild, but as aquariums gained experience in whale husbandry, this improved. Hyak lived twenty-five years, close to the twenty-nine years considered an average life expectancy for a wild male orca. A study by American researcher David Bain in the 1990s found that orcas in the better aquariums like Vancouver lived about as long as wild ones.

Since we began our work with them in 1964, killer whales have been transformed in the public mind from the despised blackfish, jackal of the ocean, to the most beloved of BC animals, an icon for all that is wild and pure in BC nature. Because of their athleticism, beauty and charisma, our killer whales tended to overshadow our other animals, in our own minds as well as the public's. They were superstars. When one went into sick bay, it made headlines. When we lost one, I don't think it is hyperbolic to say that all of Vancouver went into a period of mourning, and this was even more intense among Aquarium staff. It was like a death in the family and triggered much soul-searching about our mission. Having superstars in your cast was wonderful for bringing attention to your program, but being so dependent on one or two special animals was awkward for an organization the size the Vancouver

Killer whales' athleticism and charisma made them superstars in the Aquarium.
Ron Sangha

Below:
The Max Bell Marine Mammal Centre, completed in 1986, added a backdrop of weathered Gulf Islands' sandstone suitable for more naturalistic, educational whale shows.
Finn Larsen

Aquarium had become. Sea World dealt with this problem by establishing a self-sustaining colony of twenty or more whales all performing under the name of Shamu. This provided stability and took the spotlight off any one individual. We weren't prepared to go that route.

The killer whale program at the Vancouver Aquarium was in some ways a victim of its own success. Far from wishing the government to exterminate them with machine guns, the public now supported their most stringent protection. Capturing wild orcas was banned in BC and Washington waters, partly in response to Aquarium-assisted research that showed the coastal population to be only about 450 orcas, rather than the thousands previously thought. Some countries continued to allow wild orcas to be captured, but in keeping with rising concern about killer whale conservation, the board adopted a policy in 1992 that "the practice of collecting killer whales from wild stocks will be discontinued." Meanwhile the price of an aquarium-raised orca rose to over $1 million. It was still hoped that we could maintain our program through natural reproduction as other aquariums had done, and Bjossa successfully delivered two calves, but couldn't produce enough milk to keep them alive. That removed our last hope for keeping the killer whale program going.

In 1988 Bjossa gave birth to her first calf, the first killer whale birth ever in a Canadian aquarium.
John Ford

Do Whales Want Out?

Some argue that keeping whales in captivity is wrong because it deprives them of their freedom. These critics say captive whales should be set loose. But when Keiko, the orca that starred in the *Free Willy* movies, was really set free he didn't want to leave his familiar pen. After being forced out, he continued to seek the company of humans rather than wild whales, and after two years on his own he died. This often happens when tame animals are released to the wild. Once animals get in the habit of having their basic needs satisfied in captivity they become "habituated" and lose both the desire and the ability to live in the wild. Critics may say animals are better off if left in the wild to begin with, but most aquarists would answer that exhibiting a few rescued whales is justified if it contributes to the betterment of all whales, as it did in BC. When people spend their lives serving the greater good, we call them heroes and consider their lives well lived. Why not the same with animals?

Above: Bjossa successfully delivered two live calves at the Aquarium, but was unable to produce enough milk to keep them alive. That and other factors effectively spelled the end to the killer whale program at the Vancouver Aquarium.
Bev Ford

Left: Bjossa releases milk into the water of the whale pool during final stages of delivering a calf.
Bev Ford

LIFE WITHOUT KILLER WHALES WAS EASIER TO CONTEMPLATE owing to the fact the Vancouver Aquarium had another whale program, the beluga program. Killer whales are spectacular, but belugas (*Delphinapterus leucas*) are endearing. Their mouths are permanently curved into what looks like a smile and their white, comical heads bob up and down at the people watching them through the tank windows. The beluga's natural pace, in contrast to the orca's muscular rush, is a relaxed mosey. If there were roses in the ocean, belugas would stop to smell them. Belugas differ from orcas in far more than colouring and temperament. They have no dorsal fins, and they are surprisingly supple and flexible. They can turn their heads and twist their fatty bodies in a way impossible for the rigid, torpedo-shaped killer whales. To top it off, their foreheads bulge into a "melon" that swells and changes shape in an affecting way as the beluga examines something, as if to show its mental cogs working (actually the melon probably has more to do with navigation than thinking).

With their comical bobbing heads and mouths curved into a perpetual smile, belugas are the most endearing of whales.
Margaret Butschler

In summer, these small white whales can be found along Canada's Arctic coast, in Hudson Bay, along the Siberian and Alaskan coasts and as far south as the mouth of the St. Lawrence River on the Atlantic coast. When born, the calf is grey in colour, but as it matures it becomes snowy white. Belugas are 1.5 to 2 metres long at birth and grow to a length of about 5 metres. They eat fish such as smelt and Arctic cod but also invertebrates such as shrimp.

The first belugas to be shown by a modern aquarium were captured by the New York Aquarium in 1961. I always found them the most enjoyable animals on exhibit whenever I visited New York, and I was very interested in getting some for Vancouver. When I received word that a couple of belugas had been captured in Alaska in 1967, I flew up for a look. I found a 3.3-metre female and a 2.3-metre male moving sluggishly in the green, putrid water of a fishboat's hold. They had been lacerated in the course of being winched over the boat's rollers and needed medical attention. I got hold of Aquarium president Ralph Shaw and, as he did so many times during his years with the Aquarium, he said, "Go ahead with it, Murray." We flew them to Vancouver, put them in the old dolphin pool under the direction of our skilled veterinarians Roberta Hartman and

Left:
Female beluga Aurora arrived in 1991 and made dreams at the Aquarium come true by mothering two healthy offspring
Noel Hendrickson

Below:
Belugas are highly social animals and travel in pods of 10-20.
Margaret Butschler

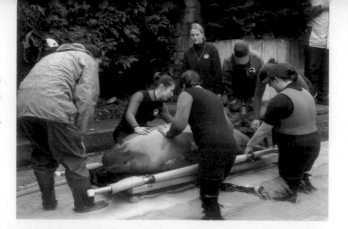

Staff at the aquarium weigh a baby beluga.
Margaret Butschler

The belugas enjoy interacting with visitors to the Aquarium and often have the last laugh.
Margaret Butschler

Alan MacNeill, and nursed them back to health. The baby beluga thrived in his new home, taking on 68.9 kilograms in three months. Whenever we fed the calf, the cow stayed right beside him, caressing and nuzzling his entire body. Every so often she would grab one of the trainer's legs with utmost care as if to say, "Be careful with my baby brother." She sometimes piggybacked him around the pool for hours at a time. She seemed quite unafraid of divers and often rubbed against their smooth wetsuits. The calf was also a gentle creature, although quite stubborn at times. One of his favourite tricks was to swim up when we were feeding his big sister and nibble on the divers' boots. He often tried to snitch a few herring from the female, until one day she blew out a big stream of bubbles at him, squealed loudly, and made a series of quick nips along his side. This apparently served as some sort of ultimate warning in beluga language, because after that the little fellow kept his distance. Belugas sometimes blow bubbles just to amuse themselves. One beluga in the Aquarium likes to blow circles of bubbles, like smoke rings, as it rests quietly on the bottom of its pool.

Lugosi, as the calf came to be known, developed the personality of a comedian and liked to spend his time at the pool viewing windows making faces at the people. Staff often commented that he seemed to be laughing at the strange creatures on the other side. Bela, the female, remained relatively timid in comparison to the sociable Lugosi. But both loved to be scratched and rubbed. Lugosi especially would roll over with a happy look on his face, inviting us to scratch his belly.

One of the most interesting things about belugas are the sounds they make. Dubbed "canaries of the sea" by old-time sailors, their vocalizations are prodigious both in variety and volume, and could be deafening if not muffled by the water. Their repertoire ranged from a high-pitched squeal, which Bela used to scold Lugosi, to a series of low-frequency clicks that were audible, even through the thick Plexiglas, as a buzzing noise. Frequently during feeding Lugosi would make a disgusted sound as if dissatisfied with his portion.

Shortly after completing the Arctic Canada Gallery in 1991, which had a spacious beluga habitat as its centrepiece, we decided to collect three more belugas from the Canadian Arctic, hoping to establish a breeding colony that would be self-sustaining. A local animal rights group challenged our permit, but it was harder to make a case against collecting belugas than against orcas because belugas are among the more abundant whales in the world and Native peoples had quotas to kill about eight hundred annually. Our three came out of these quotas, so we were actually saving them from being killed. Belugas also appear to adjust to aquarium life better than orcas, staying in good health, living to a ripe old age, and readily reproducing. Qila, born at the Aquarium in 1995, is now a healthy adult female and may one day have a calf of her own.

Belugas often seem as curious about their human observers as the humans seem about them, especially if the humans are little.
Jeff Vinnick

4
Behind the Scenes

Long renowned for the excellence of its displays and educational programs, the Vancouver Aquarium has become a true leader in the rapidly diversifying field of conservation.
Noel Hendrickson

MY OLD UBC ZOOLOGY PROFESSOR Dr. Bill Hoar gave a good description of the multiple functions the founders had in mind for the Vancouver Aquarium when he spoke at the opening of the Van Dusen Aquatic Science Centre in 1980:

"These three functions—display, education and research—are prime objectives in any great aquarium, as they are in great museums, botanical gardens and zoological parks."

Display, education and research. The first of these is the only function that most visitors to the Vancouver Aquarium see, but they see only 40 percent of the actual facility. If they could look behind the scenes at the other 60 percent, they would be surprised by how much effort it puts into the other two activities Dr. Hoar described as essential features of a great aquarium: education and research.

Having excellent displays that rivet the crowds is one thing, but as anyone who has spent much time on an aquarium floor can attest, getting people to understand what they're looking at is quite another thing. The undersea world is so foreign to most viewers, and yet so intriguing with all its strange creatures, the need for explanation or interpretation is immediately apparent. At first we didn't even have labels, other than some minimal name tags made for us by the Hudson's Bay department store on their price-tag printing machine. Then one day a middle-aged woman named Gladys Clawson

Education Director Sharon Proctor and a class of young learners at the touch pool.
The Province c. 1971

came knocking on the door. She was an artist looking for work and she was immediately put to work illustrating labels, graphics, a guidebook and education materials. She was very project-minded and productive and stayed with us for years. Later, when we did our big expansion in 1967, we hired Rudy Kovack, a gifted interior designer, to do the interior design and handle the decorative aspects of the public areas. Roderick Haig-Brown, the distinguished author and conservationist from Campbell River, BC, was engaged to write a narrative on "The Living Waters of British Columbia" that could then be transcribed on graphics throughout the local galleries.

The education program really took shape in 1967 when Dr. Sharon Proctor joined the staff as education supervisor. She was a marine biologist from Stanford University with new ideas regarding how the Aquarium could develop as a learning institution. She believed in interactive, direct observation for students and teachers. Everybody—staff, volunteers and public—got involved in education. The programs have developed to the point that in 2005 over 80,000 schoolchildren participated in Aquarium educational activities. For years most of these internationally recognized programs had been sardined into a single fifty-year-old wet lab. Classrooms, activity spaces, a new, larger wet lab and a new theatre have been on the Aquarium's ever-growing wish list for more than two decades, a dream that finally came true with the breaking of ground for the $22 million Education Centre in late 2005.

Below left:
From the beginning, the Aquarium took its role as educator of the young seriously.
*Murray Newman
c.1967*

Above:
Kathy Newman became the first docent, guiding groups around the exhibits.
*Murray Newman
c.1958*

Left:
Docents Kathy Newman and "Bays" Blackhall teach the Grade 12 Aquarium marine mammal program, 1975.
Finn Larsen

Through the first
years of the new
millennium, the
Aquarium's guiding
principle has been to
first *engage* visitors
in order to *amaze*
them so they will be
inspired to *connect*
to conservation and
sustainability.
*Left: Stephen A. Smith
/ Right: Margaret
Butschler*

RESEARCH COMPLEMENTS AN AQUARIUM'S PUBLIC ACTIVITIES in several ways. Aquariums must inform themselves as well as they can about specimens in their collections in order to keep them in good condition for display, and also to answer the myriad questions from the people who come to view them. Keeping live marine organisms over long periods also provides a prime opportunity to study their behaviour and add to the pool of scientific knowledge. Often, as in our experience with killer whales, an aquarium finds itself breaking new ground and has to acquire knowledge about a species through original research, because it isn't available from any other source. Having found ourselves in the position of being one of the leading centres of killer whale knowledge, it made sense to let our mammal scientists put their expertise at the disposal of science by undertaking field studies that went well beyond our own needs. We saw an opportunity to make an original contribution to human understanding, so we acted on it. This was in keeping with the research part of our mandate as envisioned by the founders. From the earliest days the Aquarium had strong ties with the University of British Columbia Zoology Department, which exerted its influence to ensure that the Vancouver Aquarium would be a centre of learning and education, not just entertainment. The original Aquarium building included a wet lab Dr. Hoar designed and used for his own and his students' research. More research labs were added in the 1967 expansion, allowing space to be rented to outside scientists. In 1976 the Aquarium hired its first full-time staff scientist, ichthyologist Dr. Jeff Marliave, who began studying fish and invertebrates in local waters, studies that continue as the Aquarium's core programs. In 1979, the Aquarium added a wing of lab space for marine mammals and hired a second scientist, Dr. John Ford, a UBC graduate who did pioneering research on killer whale vocalization.

Dr. John Ford, a marine mammal specialist known for his research into killer whale vocalization, became the Aquarium's second staff scientist.

Margaret Butschler

In 2001, Dr. John Ford took a position with the Department of Fisheries and Oceans at Nanaimo, BC, and carried on his work there as marine mammal biologist. The new killer whale scientist was Dr. Lance Barrett-Lennard, who received his doctorate from UBC while employed as a research associate at the Aquarium. He works as part of a team that focuses on population structure and mating patterns of killer whales through DNA analysis. Preliminary results have confirmed the clear genetic distinctiveness of resident pods who stay on the coast eating fish, and the transients, who migrate and eat mammals. Dr. Barrett-Lennard serves as co-chair of the resident killer whale recovery team operating under Canada's Species at Risk Act, which is mandated to help reverse the decline in southern resident killer whale populations. His work and that of his predecessors has established the Vancouver Aquarium as a centre of scholarly research that is respected wherever marine science is studied.

On March 24, 1989 a fully loaded supertanker, the *Exxon Valdez*, sailed out of Valdez, Alaska, and ran aground on Bligh Reef, spilling 250,000 barrels of tarry black crude oil into the pristine waters of Prince William Sound. Millions of marine creatures were oiled, including thousands of sea otters. The Vancouver Aquarium was asked for help and we dispatched our chief mammal trainer, Jeremy Fitz-Gibbon.

"We had forty-five otters in a matter of days," Jeremy said. "We got very good at removing the oil. That's an easy thing to do. Dawn detergent seemed to cut the crude oil best, so that's what we used. Getting the otter back after that is the tougher problem. They are extremely difficult to deal with. They have sensitive fur and they are difficult to house. We had great volunteers, local people, super people, but they had no idea how to handle an otter. Since I was the only person with hands-on experience at first, I was the one who organized the whole husbandry part of it. If we hadn't had the experience of sea otters in captivity, we wouldn't have saved a single one. About 500 were brought in, of which about 350 survived. It was a classic example of why we need aquariums or zoos, because nothing would be known about sea otter husbandry if it wasn't for our having these animals."

Conservation has come to dominate the Aquarium's agenda increasingly and research is essential to conservation. The Open Water Project attempts to find out why wild Steller sea lion populations in Alaska are crashing.
Noel Hendrickson

As human society spreads out and encroaches on ever more wild habitat, incidents of injured or orphaned wildlife being encountered by humans become ever more frequent. At such times, society turns desperately to experts for help, and there is nobody more expert in the business of caring for aquatic creatures than the staff of aquariums.

In January 2002, the Aquarium became involved in another wild animal rescue that captured the world's attention, this time involving a killer whale. A young female orca had turned up alone in Puget Sound often swimming beside passenger ferries going to and from Seattle. She became a great favourite of local media, who nicknamed her Springer, but Aquarium researchers identified her as A73, a two-year-old female from a well-known pod of BC whales that summered in the Johnstone Strait area three hundred kilometres north of Vancouver.

"Killer whales are highly social animals that live in family groupings so tightly knit that members are seldom out of contact with each other," Lance Barrett-Lennard says. "This fact was enough to generate concern."

Wild animal rescue is the most direct form of conservation the Aquarium undertakes. Nyac is one of hundreds of sea otters Aquarium staff helped to rescue following the *Exxon Valdez* oil spill in 1989.
Margaret Butschler

Springer was also thin and lethargic, had sloughing skin, a heavy infestation of intestinal parasites and the unhealthy smell of acetone on her breath. These factors, along with her chosen territory (a three-square-mile stretch of water with frequent vessel traffic) did not bode well for her survival. Aquarium veterinarian David Huff, Jeremy Fitz-Gibbon (now manager of the Aquarium's marine mammal rescue program) and Dr. Lance Barrett-Lennard visited Springer in early February and immediately sent a letter to the US National Marine Fisheries Service (NMFS) recommending that she be caught and temporarily confined for assessment and medical treatment, then moved back to BC waters and reintroduced to her pod. The problem was, nobody knew if her taming by humans had already gone

The Aquarium's most dramatic rescue to date involved a young killer whale named Springer.
Rolf Hicker

too far to reverse. Even if she wished to rejoin her old pod, would the wild whales allow the prodigal daughter back among them?

Springer had attained the status of a celebrity, not just in Washington state, but throughout the USA, so the idea of moving her to Canada wasn't popular. But eventually good science won out over politics and the NMFS agreed to work with the Aquarium and the Canadian Department of Fisheries and Oceans (DFO) to capture Springer and return her to the wild in Johnstone Strait.

"Springer was captured on June 13 and transferred immediately to a net-pen at Manchester, Washington, where she spent the next month being assessed, fed, rehydrated and de-wormed," reported Barrett-Lennard. "A clean bill of health led DFO to approve her for transport to BC, clearing the way for Clint Wright, the Aquarium's VP of Operations, to arrange and coordinate the details of Springer's transportation and holding."

On July 13, amid a worldwide media circus, some of it hostile, Springer was gently fitted in a stretcher that was lifted into a transport box on a high-speed catamaran for the journey from Manchester to Johnstone Strait, where she was transferred to a net-pen. Clint, Jeremy and Lance kept watch at the net-pen through the night, using a hydrophone to monitor Springer's vocalizations and breathing. Late that evening, she breached repeatedly and called loudly in response to a passing group of killer whales whose vocalizations were reminiscent of her birth pod.

The next morning Dr. Huff, Dr. John Ford of the Department of Fisheries, cetologist Graeme Ellis and Barrett-Lennard gathered to consider whether to put their daring experiment to the test and try to reunite Springer with her pod. They had all been associated with the Vancouver Aquarium's killer whale program and represented perhaps the most authoritative assemblage of killer whale experience to be found anywhere. They decided the time had come and Springer should be released as soon as members of her pod passed close to the net-pen. That opportunity came the same afternoon when the pen was approached by a subgroup of her pod. Springer was released and swam to within fifty metres of the group. The whales paused and regarded each other, but to the scientists' dismay the group headed

Springer was first placed in an enclosure where Aquarium staff helped nurse her back to health, then relocated to her home pod on the central BC coast.
Sandra Stone

east, while Springer moved west. Although Springer appeared interested in other whales, there was no initial indication that she might rejoin the pod.

"Over the next few days there was good and bad news," said Barrett-Lennard. "On a positive note, Springer associated with members of her own pod and other pods several times, and joined in social activities in Robson Bight."

On a worrisome note, she also rubbed on small boats on at least three occasions—a sign she was still relating to humans and might carry on with the behaviour that had become her pattern in Puget Sound. If word got out that Washingtonians had given up their favourite marine plaything only to have her become a pet up in Canada, the Aquarium and its scientists could be in for some real flak. The group breathed a collective sigh of relief on July 18 when Springer was observed swimming very close to A51, a sixteen-year-old female belonging to another pod. A51 was orphaned herself five years earlier and while she did not have a calf of her own, she looked after her much younger brother after their mother died, so she had mothering experience. Springer stayed with A51 for two weeks and then spent several weeks in her birth pod after striking up a relationship with a young female known as A56. Over the succeeding months Springer spent time with both A51 and A56 and stopped rubbing on boats. Four years later, Operation Springer was recognized as the world's first successful attempt to reintroduce a killer whale into the wild. Again, authorities turned to the Aquarium when faced with a wild animal rescue they were unprepared to handle themselves, and the Aquarium proved to be invaluable in resolving the situation.

Members of the 'Namgis First Nation welcome Springer as she is returned to her pod in Johnstone Strait.
Sandra Stone

Springer eventually rejoined her birth pod on the central BC coast, a historic first.
Lance Barrett-Lennard

A second orphaned killer whale calf was not so lucky. This calf, popularly known as Luna, first turned up in Nootka Sound on the west coast of Vancouver Island in the summer of 2001. It became very tame, begging for food around wharves and entertaining people on boats that were passing by. The government became concerned that it might get hurt by being accidentally struck by a boat and the Aquarium was again called in. The young bull was identified as L98, belonging to an endangered southern pod of resident orcas that ranged north to the Queen Charlotte Islands, BC, and south to Monterey Bay, California. A plan was devised to reintroduce the whale to its pod using the same techniques that proved successful with Springer, but this time politics won out over science. As in Springer's case, local residents had become attached to the friendly creature, but this time they campaigned successfully against the relocation plan. The reunion strategy was suspended and Luna continued frolicking around boats. On March 10, 2006, this habit proved fatal when it swam into the propeller of a large tugboat and was instantly killed.

Not all of the Aquarium's rescue work is so dramatic. Dr. Dave Huff, the Aquarium's long-serving veterinarian until 2006, says, "A big part of my work involved treating rescued animals. The Vancouver Aquarium's Marine Mammal Rescue Centre sees nearly one hundred marine mammals a year, mainly seals, and the majority are treated and released."

Many of the harbour seals are less than a week old. Many are malnourished or premature, some have sustained injuries in collisions with boats or have been entangled with fishing gear. Some have parasites. The pups are kept in fish totes, where they are tube-fed five times a day with a rich formula comprised of herring, salmon oil and vitamins. Although frequently hosed down, they are not kept in water to avoid chilling them. Retaining their wildness is important, so they are not handled more than necessary.

As they recover, they continue to receive veterinary care but are shifted to general care. Finally they are returned to their natural habitat—a far cry from the treatment they received in earlier eras. Before they are released they are given orange flipper tags. Most are released in groups in isolated areas in the Strait of Georgia.

The Aquarium became involved in animal rehabilitation on a much larger scale when the Species at Risk Act (SARA) was proclaimed in 2003. The act, Canada's answer to the US Endangered Species Act, specifies that a "recovery plan" must be developed as a first step for species classified as threatened or endangered. The plan's aim is to allow the species to recover to historic levels. According to the Aquarium marine mammal scientist, Dr. Lance Barrett-Lennard, "One of the reasons that the Aquarium is so well positioned to assist with recovery planning is that much of the research we do is long-term, involving the monitoring of marine species and the quality of their habitat over time." In 2004 Aquarium vice-president Clint Wright served on the sea otter recovery team, which has the task of devising strategies to save BC's threatened sea otters. Dr. Barrett-Lennard serves as co-chair of the resident killer whale recovery team, which is mandated to help reverse the decline in southern resident killer whale populations.

Dr. Dave Huff spent much of his time working with rescued animals. Here he is caring for a seal pup, which is typically the Aquarium's most common patient.
Noel Hendrickson

The Aquarium has spent many years studying the depleted lingcod populations of southern BC waters.
Phil Edgell

THE VANCOUVER AQUARIUM IN A CHANGING WORLD

Dr. John Nightingale

If you have read this book in order, you now know a lot about the Vancouver Aquarium and how it came to be what it is today. The question is, where is it going tomorrow and over the next decades? Just how does the Vancouver Aquarium fit into the world of other Aquariums?

The institution that is generally acknowledged to be the first modern public aquarium is the one that was constructed as part of the London Zoo in 1851. From that time until the 1950s and 1960s, the few aquariums that existed tended to display fish and invertebrates in isolation—much like artifacts in museum exhibits. This served a valuable purpose, since neither television nor videos nor even good colour photographs existed at the time. The only place people could see these amazing animals as they appeared underwater was in an aquarium.

Around the time the Vancouver Aquarium opened, aquariums began displaying fish and invertebrates in larger, mixed-species exhibits. This was brought about in part by technological advancements that provided larger viewing windows and improved life-support systems that could sustain larger displays, and in part because scientists began to feel that single fish displays were giving the public a distorted picture of nature.

Animals don't live by themselves; they live in groups of interdependent species in habitats defined by plants, tides, temperature, availability of light, and many other factors. This awareness was just coming to the fore when the Vancouver Aquarium opened, and through the introduction of new displays in the 1960s, it helped contribute to the development of such ecological thinking. Visitors to the Vancouver Aquarium in the 1960s were amazed by displays of mixed rockfish, bottom-dwelling fish and invertebrates living in larger displays with natural rock features, plants, and even currents or simulated tides.

The clownfish and its anenome host have a mutually beneficial relationship.
Danny Kent

Landmark events such as Earth Day in 1970 and Oceans Day in 1992 signalled a growing realization that while all animals on earth and in the ocean live in mixed groups and habitats, no animal lives completely independent of the influence of humans. Humans now have such a pervasive influence on the natural world that they impact every square inch of earth and ocean, often interrupting or otherwise altering evolutionary processes. Humans have overfished 90 percent of the world's commercial fish species. Over 90 percent of animals (whales and fish) over six feet in length are now gone from the world's oceans (Meyer, 2004). We—humans and the ecosystems we depend on—are now co-evolving at a rate unprecedented in history.

We don't have a nature problem, we have a people problem. It is people who have caused the problems, and only people can begin to make the personal and societal changes that will ensure our grandchildren have a BC, Canada and world to use and enjoy that is at least as good as it is today.

Beginning in the early 1990s, the Vancouver Aquarium helped lead the next revolution. The organization realized it could no longer be content with displaying marine animals as curiosities or even showing them in simulated natural habitats. It was one of the first to recognize that aquariums need to be a force in raising public awareness and mobilizing the desire to participate in sustainability and conservation. Helping people become part of the solution, not the problem, now guides almost everything the Aquarium does.

This is a fitting legacy to an organization with a strong history of leadership. The Vancouver Aquarium is credited with having introduced the first live interpreters in general display (Taylor, 1995). Before the 1960s, visitors found plenty of printed graphic labels telling them what the animals were, and a few

Almost too late, researchers found the unassuming rockfish may live for over 100 years, making it slow to regenerate and susceptible to overfishing.
Margaret Butschler

Sea horses are like fairy tale creatures come to life. They flirt, dance, change colour and mate for life, and the male rears the eggs in his pouch. Because they are overfished, the Aquarium has been researching ways of adapting them to aquaculture in order to relieve pressure on wild populations.
Margaret Butschler

interpretive graphic panels expanding on some of the "natural" stories emanating from the particular display. With interpreters present in the public galleries, visitors could interact with them and exercise their curiosity by asking questions. Visitors generally became much more active and interested in their visit. Today, the Aquarium is known for its innovative use of new and digital technology to assist in engaging visitors and expanding interpretation, and for the development of public programs that extend that engagement into nature.

Throughout the 1990s and through the first decade of the new millennium, the guiding principle for visitors has evolved into the clear promise that we will first *engage* each of our visitors in order to *amaze* them because we want to *inspire* them so that we can *connect* them to conservation and sustainability. This chronology of "conservation learning" begins with raising awareness,

The Ocean Project

In 1993, Dr. John Nightingale, President of the Vancouver Aquarium joined together with the directors of the New York Aquarium, the Shedd Aquarium (Chicago), the National Aquarium (Baltimore), the Monterey Bay Aquarium (California) and the New England Aquarium (Boston) to found The Ocean Project (TOP). The question was "how can we raise public awareness of and concern about the oceans to the level that has been achieved for rainforests, without taking twenty-five years to do it?"

In 1995, TOP conducted the first US / Canada-wide polls on public awareness, interest and concern for the oceans. The polls found high levels of interest (over 90 percent), strong concern for the future of the oceans (over 90 percent), but almost zero understanding (real knowledge) of the problems or what the solutions might be.

Through the late 1990s up to 2005, TOP's focus was to develop new ways of communicating the key issues to public audiences. Workshops were held to learn from educators and educational psychologists, learning specialists, mass marketing experts and others with any expertise – no matter what field they came from. The resulting "tool box" of new communications methods toured North American aquariums and other partner institutions, often with personal presentations and workshops by the Vancouver Aquarium's Vice-President of Education, Patrick O'Callaghan, who became well known in aquarium circles.

By 2006, TOP had become a network of over 600 aquariums, university biology departments, a variety of government (both federal, state and local) agencies, and a number of conservation NGOs (non-governmental organizations). Another poll will be conducted in 2006 to assess change and to plot strategy for the next decade. Since well over 100 million North Americans visit aquariums and other partner organizations each year, the TOP leadership team (which still includes the Vancouver Aquarium) is now planning how the contact the partner organizations and institutions have with the general public can be better directed. And, perhaps more importantly, TOP's focus is on working with a wide cross-section of conservation thinkers and strategists on the key goals for improving the long-term prospects for sustainable oceans and ocean life.

stimulating curiosity and then concern, which then brings people to an accessible starting point from which they can become involved. Each year hundreds of schoolchildren take part in the annual Goodbye Salmon Fry Celebration, when thousands of juvenile salmon are released into the BC Hydro Salmon Stream to begin their three-year migration into the Pacific Ocean and back. In the fall many more visitors come back to see adult fish return to their home creek to spawn, enjoying a ringside view of one of nature's most impressive spectacles. People inspired by this experience become good candidates to participate in the Aquarium's TD Canada Trust Great Canadian Shoreline Cleanup, which saw 36,798 volunteers remove a total of 86,201 kg of harmful debris from 1,477 km of shoreline in 2005.

Aquariums, and the Vancouver Aquarium in particular, have moved from being tourist attractions, or attractions augmented by helping the school system with assisted learning, to being true leaders in the many rapidly growing and diversifying conservation fields. Leadership means being aware of what is happening in nature, what is happening in the community, and the very hard work of doing something about the problems and issues. Some of the work is communications based, some is engagement or emotional contact, and some is organizational in providing people with a personal avenue for action. The Vancouver Aquarium is considered a leader in each of these areas. It isn't easy, the goals are sometime not completely clear, yet the work to be done to sustain our aquatic and ocean environments is far more important today than it was fifty years ago. That is the Aquarium's vision and mission—to do everything the organization can possibly do to ensure future generations know and enjoy a natural world at least as productive and complete as it is today.

The Aquarium's vision and mission is to do everything it can to assure that future generations know and enjoy a natural world at least as productive and complete as it is today.
Lance Barrett-Lennard

Harbour Publishing Co. Ltd.
P.O. Box 219, Madeira Park, BC, V0N 2H0
www.harbourpublishing.com

Special thanks are due to Treva Ricou, Margaret Butschler, Hans Sipma, Joy Hayden, Jeremy Fitz-Gibbon,
Dr. Lance Barrett-Lennard, Dr. John Ford and Kathy Newman.

This book is dedicated to the 34 million people who have voted with their feet in support of the Vancouver
Aquarium over the years.

Page and cover design by Roger Handling, Terra Firma Digital Arts
Cover image by Noel Hendrickson
Production and image editing by Vici Johnstone
Scanning by Agile Media

Printed and bound in Canada

Harbour Publishing acknowledges financial support from the Government of Canada through the Book
Publishing Industry Development Program and the Canada Council for the Arts, and from the Province of
British Columbia through the British Columbia Arts Council and the Book Publisher's Tax Credit through
the Ministry of Provincial Revenue.

THE CANADA COUNCIL | LE CONSEIL DES ARTS
FOR THE ARTS | DU CANADA
SINCE 1957 | DEPUIS 1957

BRITISH
COLUMBIA
ARTS COUNCIL
Supported by the Province of British Columbia

Library and Archives Canada Cataloguing in Publication

Newman, Murray A., 1924-
    People, fish and whales : the Vancouver Aquarium story / Murray
Newman.
ISBN 1-55017-382-0

    1. Vancouver Aquarium—History. I. Title.
QL79.C22V35 2006   597'.07371133   C2006-900986-4